Here Comes the Fireboat

ELK GROVE
PRESS, INC.

The author and illustrator

wish to thank Captain Trygve

Thorsen and Cal Egerton of the

Los Angeles Fire Department,

for their cooperation and

assistance in the preparation of

this book.

Here Comes the Fireboat

by Lillian Colonius

illustrated with photographs
by Glenn W. Schroeder

Elk Grove Press, Chicago, Los Angeles

Fireboats are a special and exciting part of a city's fire department. They fight fires in ships, on docks or wharfs, and in buildings along the water front.

Fireboats are always ready to go out into harbors, lakes, and rivers. These firemen and fireboats work in a large harbor. Their firehouse is on the harbor.

The firehouse has offices, living quarters and work rooms for the men. The fireboat stays in one end of the firehouse. It is tied up in a place called a slip.

Each firehouse has a captain and a crew. The men in the crew have different duties. One man is a pilot and one is the first mate. Others are engineers, deck firemen and scuba divers. You may be surprised to learn what scuba divers do on a fireboat!

Each crew works for twenty-four hours. They must be ready to answer the fire alarm day and night. While they are on duty the men eat and sleep in the firehouse.

The firemen have their own kitchen which they call a galley. They have their meals here. All of the men take turns cooking. Sometimes they become very good cooks!

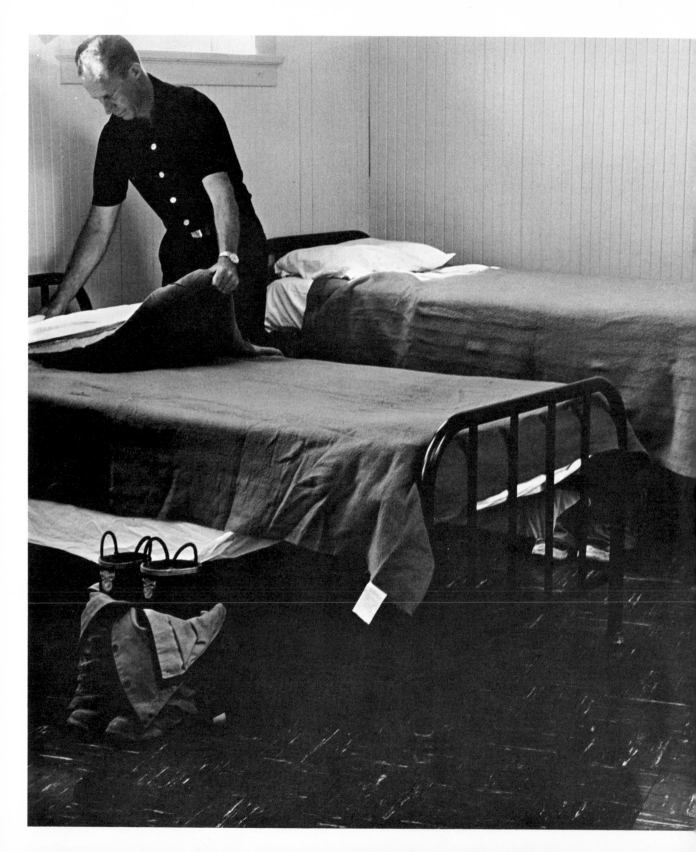

Many of the firemen like to rest after dinner. In the recreation room they may watch television, read, or study. Often they play a fast game of handball outdoors. Everyone is always listening in case the fire bell rings.

Even when a fireman goes to bed he is ready for the alarm. He may have to get dressed quickly so he keeps his boots and pants beside him. His coat and helmet hang on a hook near the fireboat.

Loud alarms awaken the men when there is a fire at night. They jump into their boots and pants, grab their helmets and coats, and rush off in the boat to fight the fire.

The firemen begin their work at eight o'clock every morning. They line up in front of the captain for inspection. The captain gives them their orders for the day.

Firemen go to class, too. The class is called a company drill. The captain is the teacher. Fireboat crews study new ways to fight fires. Sometimes the captain draws pictures of new equipment on the blackboard. Each man must learn to use the equipment.

Today the captain wants to have a fire fighting drill. The crew will go out into the harbor on the boat. They will practice spraying water and foam. They have some new monitors to test. The captain wants to see how far they will spray water.

When class ends the firemen prepare for their fire fighting drill. The men must change their uniforms and put on work clothes.

Deck firemen call their work clothes "turn-outs." They wear heavy canvas coats over their blue denim clothes. The scuba divers put on rubber suits, face masks, and helmets. Each diver carries an air tank on his back.

Soon everyone is ready. Each man takes his place on the boat. The deck firemen toss off the ropes and the fireboat is ready to move out into the harbor. The bow lookout fireman runs to the front of the boat to see if the way is clear. In foggy weather he never leaves the bow of the boat. He must watch for other boats and listen for their fog horns. If danger is near he signals to the pilot.

The pilot house is on the deck of the fireboat. It has windows on four sides so the pilot can see all around him.

The pilot has many ways to guide the boat. He uses a compass to find directions — north, south east, west. A radar screen shows objects he cannot see when it is foggy or dark. The radar screen shows things which are too far away to be seen by the bow look-out man.

At night the pilot turns on spot lights and search lights. When the boat is going to a fire he sounds the siren to warn other ships of the danger.

The pilot turns a big wheel to steer the boat. He uses an enunciator to send orders to the engine room. On the enunciator there is a dial with the words "ahead," "astern," and "stop." To start the boat the pilot pulls the handle of the enunciator. It points to "ahead." Then the hand on the enunciator in the engine room moves to "ahead." Now the engineers know where to move the throttles for the engines.

compass

radar

enunciator

Behind the pilot house is the nozzle room. Sometimes it is called the Gold Room. The brass nozzles shine like gold.

Fireboats have nozzles of many different sizes. The firemen must be careful to use the right sized nozzle for the fire they are fighting. Some of the nozzles send a small stream of water.

They will not put out a big fire. Nozzles with a big stream might overturn a small boat.

A nozzle and hose is too heavy for the firemen to hold. The pressure behind the water in the hose makes it hard to handle. The firemen have to use clamps to fasten the hose to the boat railing. They call the clamp a "standee." The standee holds the hose so the firemen can turn the nozzle on the fire.

Some of the firemen in the crew are engineers. They climb down a ladder into the engine room. The engine room is inside the stern, the back part of the boat. It is a very busy place!

Some of the fireboat's engines move the boat through the water. Two engineers watch gauges and push throttles to run these engines.

Other engines pump water from the harbor for the fire hoses. The water comes up from underneath the boat through large pipes.

The captain and the pilot give orders to the engineers. They signal when to start and stop the engines. The captain tells an engineer how much water is needed to fight the fire. Sometimes the water must be shut off quickly. Then a red light comes on and a bell rings.

It is very hot in the engine room. The fireboat must have blowers to draw air from ventilators on the deck. The fresh air cools the men.

When all the engines are running they are noisy. The engineers have covers for their ears to shut out the noise.

Now the engines are ready to go. The pilot is at the wheel. The captain gives the order to start moving out into the harbor.

The men have many jobs to do to get ready for the drill. They must have all of their equipment ready.

Some of the men lay out the hose and connect it to pipes. The pipes are called manifolds. They carry water pumped from the harbor.

On top of the fireboat is a tower which can be moved high up into the air. The nozzle mounted on the tower shoots a stream of water into fires. These mounted nozzles are sometimes called water guns.

Have you guessed why some of the firemen are scuba divers? The answer is very simple.

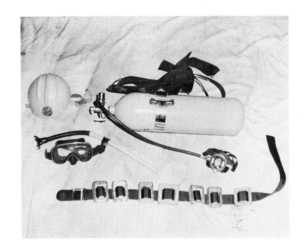

Fires often begin under wharves and spread to buildings and ships. Before scuba divers joined the crew, the only way the firemen could get under the wharves was to go in small boats. Heavy smoke and heat made it very difficult to fight these fires.

Some of the firemen knew how to scuba dive. They showed their captain how helpful they could be. Plans were made to train more firemen to be scuba divers.

These men go to scuba diving schools. They learn about diving equipment and how to take care of it. In fire fighting drills they practice wearing their diving gear. Just as a deck fireman wears a helmet, a scuba diver wears a special hard helmet. Before the divers jump into the water, other firemen give their gear a safety check.

Scuba divers have special equipment to help them fight fires. This special help is a floating monitor. Water is pumped through the hose to the nozzle in the middle of the monitors.

Plastic bottles hold the hose and keep it from sinking. The monitors are fastened to the hose about ten feet apart. The divers swim along with the monitors to guide them under wharves and spray water to keep the fire from spreading.

When the men are diving, a red flag with a white stripe flys over the fireboat. This warns other boats to stay away. The propellors of other boats would be dangerous to the divers.

Scuba divers can work in the thick smoke under the wharves because the tanks on their backs supply them with fresh air. The cold water of the harbor protects them from the fire's heat.

The deck firemen on the boat turn their turret guns
to sweep water across the wharves. By turning wheels
on the sides of the turrets, firemen can shoot the water
into the fire. The fireboat looks like a fountain when
all of the water guns and hoses are spraying water into
the air.

The firemen must be ready to answer special alarms like oil and gasoline fires. They spray foam instead of water on these fires. The foam piles up and puts out the fire. Fire cannot burn without air and foam keeps air from getting to the fire.

Sometimes the men are called to prevent a fire. Gasoline or oil spilled on the water is called a "slick." It is dangerous because it burns easily and quickly. The firemen rush to oil or gasoline "slicks" before a fire can begin. They spray streams of water on the slick to spread it out. The boat's propellors churn up the water to help break up the dangerous slick.

The firemen do not always use their big fireboat to fight fires. Some harbor fires are very small. The large fireboat with all of its equipment is not needed.

The firehouse has a smaller boat manned by a crew of three.

Sometimes the small boat helps the big fireboat at fires. The small boat can bring more equipment to a fire. It may be able to move closer to a burning ship to put firemen aboard. The small boat can take injured people or firemen away from fires. Often, it can break up the "spills" of gasoline or oil floating on the water.

The first mate runs the small boat. Two firemen are deck hands. There are two engines on board. One engine drives the boat and the other pumps water. The hoses and fire fighting equipment are kept in boxes under the seats and decks of this boat.

When the drill is over the boat returns to the firehouse. The pilot backs the fireboat into the slip. The firemen catch the ropes to tie the boat. They slip them around mooring bitts on board. These are brass posts on the deck of the boat.

The fireboat has safely returned, but the men have not finished their work. Now they must clean the equipment. First, the men wash everything on the deck with fresh water. Then they wash away the harbor water in the nozzles and hose. This is an important job because the harbor water is very salty. It will "corrode" or damage the metal if not quickly rinsed off. Other metal parts of the boat and equipment are also cleaned with fresh water.

The fire hoses are hung in the tower to dry and dry hoses are put in their place. Now the firemen begin polishing the equipment. It takes many hours of rubbing until the metal is clean and shining again.

When the men are not fighting fires or drilling, they work on the boats and firehouse to keep them in good condition. They scrape the old paint and rust from the boat and paint it. They scrub the decks, clean the engines, wash windows and do many other chores.

There is always work to do at the firehouse, but there is time for the men to rest and relax — while they wait for the fire alarm to sound.